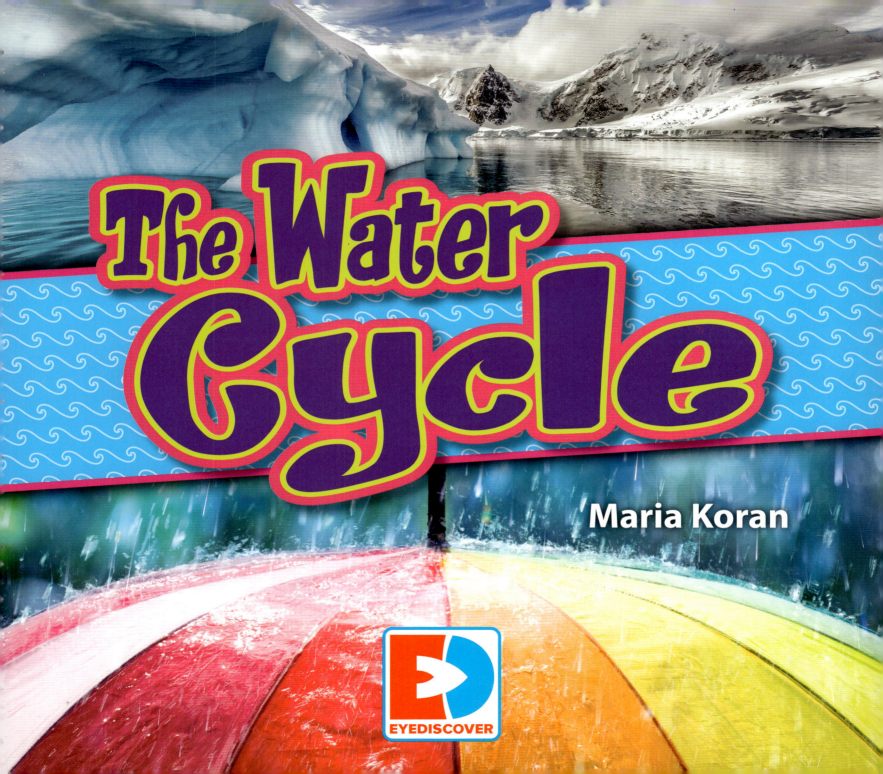

The Water Cycle

Maria Koran

EYEDISCOVER

EYEDISCOVER

Go to **www.eyediscover.com** and enter this book's unique code.

BOOK CODE

AVN95986

EYEDISCOVER brings you optic readalongs that support active learning.

Published by AV² by Weigl
350 5ᵗʰ Avenue, 59ᵗʰ Floor New York, NY 10118
Website: www.eyediscover.com

Library of Congress Cataloging-in-Publication Data available on request

ISBN 978-1-7911-0776-5 (hardcover)

Printed in Guangzhou, China
1 2 3 4 5 6 7 8 9 0 23 22 21 20 19

072019
121818

Project Coordinator: John Willis
Designer: Mandy Christiansen and Sushant Deshpande

Weigl acknowledges Alamy and iStock as the primary image suppliers for this title.

EYEDISCOVER provides enriched content, optimized for tablet use, that supplements and complements this book. EYEDISCOVER books strive to create inspired learning and engage young minds in a total learning experience.

I am a lion.

Watch
Video content brings each page to life.

Browse
Thumbnails make navigation simple.

Read
Follow along with text on the screen.

Listen
Hear each page read aloud.

Your EYEDISCOVER Optic Readalongs come alive with...

Audio
Listen to the entire book read aloud.

Video
High resolution videos turn each spread into an optic readalong.

OPTIMIZED FOR

 TABLETS

 **WHITEBOARDS**

 COMPUTERS

✓ **AND MUCH MORE!**

The Water Cycle

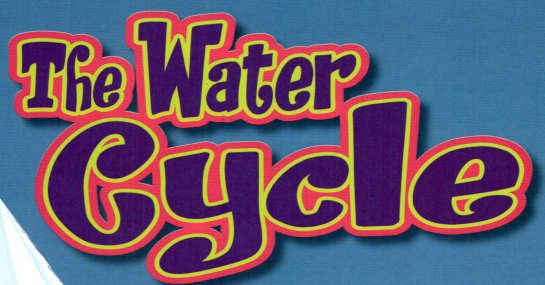

In this book, you will learn about

- **what it is**

- **how it works**

- **what it does**

and much more!

Without water, there would be no life on Earth.

The water we use comes from places such as oceans, lakes, and rivers.

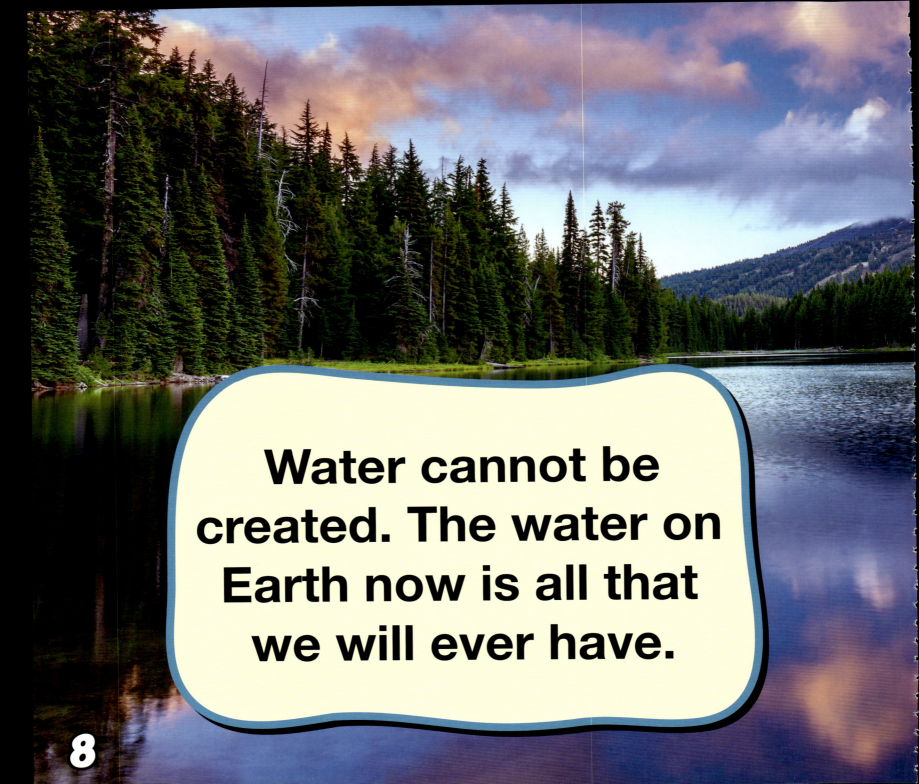

Water cannot be created. The water on Earth now is all that we will ever have.

Water can be found in different forms. It can be ice, snow, or rain.

When water in nature changes form, it is known as the water cycle.

Heat from the Sun warms water. It makes water turn into clouds.

When water in clouds cools, it falls. This makes rain or snow.

The rain or snow that falls on the ground can make lakes or rivers.

Protecting Earth's water is important. We need to keep water clean of garbage and chemicals.

THE WATER CYCLE FACTS

About **90 percent** of water in the air comes from oceans, lakes, and rivers.

A person can only **live** for about **a week** without water.

Less than **1 percent** of Earth's water can be used for drinking.

About **30 percent** of the **rain and snow** that falls in the United States ends up in **streams, lakes, or oceans.**

Mount Waialeale, Hawai'i, is one of the rainiest places on Earth. It gets about **450 inches** of rain each year. **(1,140 centimeters)**

About **71 percent** of Earth is covered in **water**.

KEY WORDS

Research has shown that as much as 65 percent of all written material published in English is made up of 300 words. These 300 words cannot be taught using pictures or learned by sounding them out. They must be recognized by sight. This book contains 42 common sight words to help young readers improve their reading fluency and comprehension. This book also teaches young readers several important content words, such as proper nouns. These words are paired with pictures to aid in learning and improve understanding.

Page	Sight Words First Appearance
4	be, Earth, life, no, on, there, water, without, would
7	and, as, comes, from, places, rivers, such, the, use, we
8	all, have, is, now, that, will
11	can, different, found, in, it, or
12	changes, when
14	into, makes, turn
17	this
20	important, keep, need, of, to

Page	Content Words First Appearance
7	lakes, oceans
11	forms, ice, rain, snow
12	water cycle
14	clouds, heat, Sun
17	rain, snow
19	ground
20	chemicals, garbage

I am a lion.

Watch
Video content brings each page to life.

Browse
Thumbnails make navigation simple.

Read
Follow along with text on the screen.

Listen
Hear each page read aloud.

EYEDISCOVER

Go to www.eyediscover.com and enter this book's unique code.

BOOK CODE

AVN95986